Hometown Memories II

People and places in Litchfield County, Greater Waterbury, the Naugatuck Valley and beyond

Presented by the

RepublicanAmerican

Waterbury, Connecticut

Acknowledgments

The Republican-American and Sunday Republican are pleased to present *Hometown Memories II*.

This unique book is the result of contributions made by many people and organizations from throughout our readership area.

We are indebted to early residents who captured their times – our history – in photographs. And we're all indebted to the many individuals who are committed to preserving our history in various libraries, archives and personal collections all around this area we call home.

In addition to precious selections from family albums of many of our readers, we also received the generous contribution of time and photo archives from the following organizations:

Cheshire Historical Society

Mattatuck Museum

Naugatuck Historical Society

Old Bethlem Historical Society

Southbury Historical Society

Southington Historical Society

Torrington Historical Society

Watertown Historical Society

Woodbury Public Library

On the cover

The image on the cover is a photo illustration using a number of images found in this book.

Contents

Foreword

"Difficult times have helped me to understand better than before, how infinitely rich and beautiful life is in every way, and that so many things that one goes worrying about are of no importance whatsoever..."
— Isak Dinesen, Danish writer

It was a time of change in Greater Waterbury and the Litchfield Hills between the two world wars. Since then, the village greens and small town atmosphere of Litchfield County has changed little, but for those communities along the Naugatuck River, life would never be the same. The general store concept in many of the smaller villages was still there – the country doctor, the farms, the one-room school house and horse power, when it really was that – but the river provided fuel for industry.

It was the river towns of Torrington, Waterbury, Thomaston, Naugatuck and Seymour that were caught up in the Industrial Revolution. The rise in industry brought immigrants from Europe to man the factories. Waterbury went from just over 51,000 people in 1900 to just under 100,000 by 1940. The other industrial centers saw similar growth. The smaller towns, however, remained much as they were, save for a few conveniences of the times.

This was when the brass industry took hold, rooted in Waterbury, but branching into Torrington and Thomaston as well. Chase Brass and Copper, Scovill and American Brass alone employed thousands. Then there was clock-making – Waterbury Clock, Lux, Seth Thomas – while in Naugatuck, there was U.S. Rubber, which employed as many as 6,000 in its heyday turning out U.S. Keds, the sneaker every youngster in America had to have on his/her feet. Some 50,000 people eventually went to work in Greater Waterbury's industries, while Torrington factories employed 10,000.

In fact, Waterbury, according to Collier's Encyclopedia, was one of the nation's 20 most important industrial areas during the '40s.

With the industry that fueled the growth in the first half century, came the captains of industry, who developed enough wealth to build some of the mansions that still stand in Waterbury's Overlook section. Many of the historic buildings that line Grand Street and lower Bank Street were constructed during this period. The Church of the Immaculate Conception and the Elton Hotel on the Green gave downtown a touch of class.

With the arrival of talking pictures, great movie palaces were built – The State, the Strand, the Plaza and the Palace in downtown Waterbury and the Warner in Torrington – while many of the neighborhoods had their own smaller theaters. Even small towns like Thomaston, Oakville and Winsted had theaters that showed movies nightly. And in the smallest towns, motion pictures could be seen at a town hall or school.

Talkies brought an end to vaudeville, which in turn yielded the closings and demolition of the Alhambra in Torrington and Jacques Opera

House in downtown Waterbury. Rosalind Russell recalled sneaking away from her parents to the Jacques before she went to Hollywood to become a motion picture star of the '40s and '50s.

The automobile was still in its infancy, and for most, it was the trolley or bus that provided transportation. The majority of people lived within walking distance of their jobs. That explains the tightly packed neighborhoods around what once were major employers in Waterbury, Naugatuck and Torrington. In fact, it was the factory whistle that woke the natives and another that told them it was time to report to work. Because of the short walking distances, workers usually went home for lunch. Employers had no need of parking lots because only a handful drove to work. Housing on a trolley or bus line was much sought after.

For those who did drive, the car was for Sunday – an afternoon ride in the country, a baseball game at Hamilton Park or a visit to grandma's. There were no interstates, so even a short trip to a nearby town could be an adventure. The journey between the downtowns of Waterbury and Torrington, for example, was an hour's ride.

Without the automobile, it was mom and pop groceries, bake shops and the butcher that provided the wares for the day. Even in tightly packed Waterbury, many had backyard gardens, while others raised chickens. Neighbors could buy eggs or slaughtered chickens. The milkman delivered, usually twice a week.

Because of such neighborhood commerce, even the smallest towns were pretty much self-contained. It was a time when you married the girl next door or at least someone from the same town. In the smaller towns and in the neighborhoods – there were few secrets – everybody knew everybody.

The daily newspapers or a few minutes of radio news were the main sources of information from the outside world. Radio brought Jack Benny, Fred Allen and Fred Waring to millions of American living rooms across the nation.

From the Roaring 20s and bathtub gin, when everybody was living it up, sprang the Great Depression. Almost overnight, bread lines formed to provide food for the unemployed. Waterbury and neighboring towns had work farms where the needy could live and provide for themselves and their families until they could get back on their feet. Waterbury's farm was the Brookside Home, which is now Brookside Road, while in Torrington it was in the area of John Brown's birthplace. Even Salisbury had the Town Asylum. Most of these farms were funded by private individuals or businesses.

After the end of the Great War, Americans didn't care to get involved in the turmoil developing in Europe, but that only led to a greater disaster when the Japanese bombed Pearl Harbor. World War II brought an end to the Depression, and ushered in an era of prosperity to Northwestern Connecticut.

CHAPTER ONE
Views and Street Scenes

*"When strangers start acting like neighbors...
communities are reinvigorated."*

— Ralph Nader, Winsted native

Europeans of the 19th century saw America as a place where the streets were lined with gold. Obviously that was not so, but many buildings from the late 19th and early 20th centuries, especially in Waterbury, could not be built today. They would not be cost effective, and the immigrant talent necessary to build such palaces has all but vanished.

Redevelopment and the Great Flood of 1955 took many of those fine buildings, but some remain, especially on Grand and lower Bank streets. For most, what is left are only photographs.

Downtown, not only in Waterbury, but in all cities, was where everything happened. There were no malls or strip plazas, only trolley and bus lines that congregated at Exchange Place in Waterbury and Center Square in Torrington.

What the 55 flood didn't take, redevelopment did, especially on West Main Street and Union Street in the downtown area of Waterbury.

The flood changed Naugatuck and Winsted the most; 60 years later, Winsted is still struggling, while in Naugatuck, there are ambitious plans for a complete downtown overhaul. It wasn't so much the flood, but economics that changed Seymour when the huge vacant industrial complex along the river was torn down to make room for a supermarket, and the new, elevated Route 8 sliced through downtown. Except for the buildings that straddled the Naugatuck River, Torrington is much the same, though for the hordes of Thursday night shoppers that visited the now defunct Mertz, McCann's and Bronson King's are no longer there.

LEFT: The Bank and South Main intersection, Waterbury, circa 1922.
Courtesy Republican-American archives

RIGHT: A view of the Green in Waterbury, circa 1920.   *Courtesy Republican-American archives*

ABOVE: View of South Street from the Green in Litchfield, 1920. *Courtesy Robert Doyle*

ABOVE: A view of Main and Davis streets, Oakville, looking south, circa 1920. *Courtesy Watertown Historical Society*

RIGHT: South Main Street in Cheshire, circa 1920. *Courtesy Cheshire Historical Society*

ABOVE: Exchange Place as seen from the intersection of Bank and South Main streets, Waterbury, circa 1922. *Courtesy Republican-American archives*

ABOVE LEFT: View at the corner of South Main and Maple streets, Naugatuck, circa 1921. Many of these buildings were destroyed by the 1955 flood. Others were removed to make way for Route 8 overpass. *Courtesy Naugatuck Historical Society*

LEFT: A view of the Green in Waterbury, looking east, circa 1920. *Courtesy Republican-American archives*

ABOVE: Bank and Center streets, Waterbury, circa 1925. *Courtesy Republican-American archives*

LEFT: Overhead view of Bank and Grand streets, looking north toward the Green, Waterbury, circa 1922. *Courtesy Republican-American archives*

ABOVE: Street scene in Naugatuck, circa 1920s. *Courtesy Republican-American archives*

LEFT: Exchange Place, Waterbury, 1920s. *Courtesy Republican-American archives*

ABOVE: A view of North Street, looking south, Litchfield, circa 1925.
Courtesy Republican-American archives

RIGHT: A view of businesses at the Scovill and South Main streets intersection, Waterbury, 1920s. *Courtesy Republican-American archives*

BELOW: South Main Street, at the intersection of East Clay and West Clay streets, Waterbury, 1928. *Courtesy Mattatuck Museum*

ABOVE: A view of Maple Street from the Green, Naugatuck, January 1936.
Courtesy Republican-American archives

ABOVE: The Brown Block at the corner of East and South Main streets, Waterbury. This is one of the last photos taken of this Exchange Place vista before face-lifting began in the summer of 1930.
Courtesy Republican-American archives

LEFT: Main Street at Laurence Square, Torrington, 1930s.
Courtesy Republican-American archives

RIGHT: A busy Bank Street looking north in Waterbury, circa 1935. *Courtesy Republican-American archives*

BELOW: A view of Freight Street, Chase Parkway and Riverside Street, December 18, 1936. *Courtesy Republican-American archives*

ABOVE: Main Street, Derby, 1936. *Courtesy Republican-American archives*

ABOVE: East Main and Cherry streets. Waterbury, December 17, 1936. The motorcycle policeman is identified as John McWeeney. *Courtesy Republican-American archives*

LEFT: South Main Street and Washington Avenue, Waterbury, December 1936.
Courtesy Republican-American archives

ABOVE: Main Street, Winsted, March 1936.
Courtesy Republican-American archives

LEFT: A view of Baldwin and Mill streets, Waterbury, January 1937. *Courtesy Republican-American archives*

BELOW: View of Seymour, June 1936.
Courtesy Republican-American archives

ABOVE: Baldwin and Washington streets, Waterbury, January 1937.
Courtesy Republican-American archives

RIGHT: Canal street, Shelton, circa 1939.
Courtesy Republican-American archives

ABOVE: The clock in the Green decorated for Christmas, 1939. *Courtesy Republican-American archives*

RIGHT: Clearing snow on Bank Street, Waterbury, 1939. *Courtesy Republican-American archives*

RIGHT: A view of Prospect, March 1939.
Courtesy Republican-American archives

ABOVE: Hospital Road in Southbury, April 1939.
Courtesy Republican-American archives

LEFT: North Main Street looking south to Main Street, Thomaston, circa 1939. *Courtesy Republican-American archives*

RIGHT: A view of South Britain, 1939. *Courtesy Republican-American archives*

CHAPTER TWO
Main Street Thrives

*"After all, the chief business of the
American people is business."*

— Calvin Coolidge

From the 1920s to the early 1960s, downtown was the place to be. Main streets in Torrington, New Milford, Waterbury, and Naugatuck teemed with crowds of shoppers, eager to examine the newest dry goods at Howland-Hughes and other fine department stores. The venerable five-and-dimes: Newbury's, Woolworth's and W.T. Grant held sway in the bigger cities while local shop keepers such as Fuller's in Thomaston were mainstays. Mertz, McCann's, and JC Penney's were the Main Street beacons in Torrington.

Small towns and villages relied on general stores where one could buy gloves, candy, shovels or order a funeral suit. Few would have imagined so much infrastructure giving way to mega shopping malls such as the Brass Mill Center, with acres of stores and even more acres of parking. While it's difficult to recapture the feeling of those days, hints of it do remain along Main streets in Watertown and Thomaston and West Street in Litchfield.

Most folks walked to the store or made a once-a-week expedition to the city. Separate stops were required at the butcher, the baker, the cobbler, the drugstore and the hardware store. In Waterbury, the only hardware survivor is Schmidt's and Serafine's, which had to move from its downtown location in the name of urban renewal. Night clubs flourished as did movie theaters. Newspapers hung up headlines and afternoon baseball scores in their front windows.

LEFT: Waterbury Hotel, West Main Street, June 1936. *Courtesy Republican-American archives*

RIGHT: A Waterbury Democrat employee takes down information brought in by these young men in 1924. *Courtesy Republican-American archives*

ABOVE: Main Street Garage, Woodbury, known locally as Carl and Walt's, circa 1920. Pictured in front of the garage, from left are Miss Allen, Dick Kitney, Joe Lyons, Walt Griswold, Nick Anderson, Carl Anderson and Bill Williams.
Courtesy Woodbury Public Library

RIGHT: W.J. Pape turns the first shovel for the new Republican-American building, Leavenworth Street, Printers Court, March 13, 1924. *Courtesy Republican-American archives*

ABOVE: Merchants Trust Co., Waterbury, December 22, 1931. *Courtesy Republican-American archives*

RIGHT: The original sales office for Soule-Roberts for lakeside lots in Southbury near what is now Exit 14 on I-84.
Courtesy Southbury Historical Society Archives

ABOVE: South End Pharmacy on South Main Street, Torrington, circa 1927. Moses Doyle, Jr., purchased this business in 1923 and moved to a new building across the street in 1928. He also changed the name to Doyle's Pharmacy. *Courtesy Robert Doyle*

LEFT: The Waterbury Democrat composing room in the 1920s.
Courtesy Republican-American archives

FAR LEFT: Construction work continues on Moses Doyle's pharmacy at 237 South Main Street, Torrington, circa 1927. *Courtesy Robert Doyle*

ABOVE: Inside of Ortone's Pastry Shop, 293 South Main Street, Waterbury, 1929. *Courtesy Mattatuck Museum*

ABOVE: A Citizens Coal Co. delivery truck in front of Angelo's Grocery on North Main Street in Waterbury, circa 1928. *Courtesy Mattatuck Museum*

RIGHT: Moses Doyle, Jr., father of Robert Doyle, in his pharmacy at 237 South Main in Torrington, circa 1928. Moses Doyle, Jr., purchased the South End Pharmacy in 1923. He occupied a building across the street for five years before moving and changing the name to Doyle's Pharmacy in 1928. *Courtesy Robert Doyle*

LEFT: Exterior of the Waterbury Hotel, Waterbury, West Main Street, circa 1929. *Courtesy Republican-American archives*

ABOVE & LEFT: Interior of Doyle's Pharmacy at 237 South Main Street, Torrington, circa 1929. The pharmacy also housed a sub-station selling stamps and accepting packages for mailing. *Courtesy Robert Doyle*

RIGHT: Businesses line West Main Street, near Exchange Place in Waterbury, circa 1930. *Courtesy Republican-American archives*

ABOVE: Blue Ribbon Garage on West Main Street in Waterbury, circa 1931.
Courtesy Marilyn Browne Mastin

ABOVE: Melbourne Gas Station on Bridge Street, Union City, 1930s. *Courtesy Naugatuck Historical Society*

RIGHT: Interior of Canfield's Drug Store (H.H. Canfield Corner Drug Store), Woodbury, early 1930s. Included in the photo are Henry Canfield and Willy Aguilar. *Courtesy Bob Cowles*

LEFT: The Elton Hotel, Waterbury, 1936. In 1903-04, prominent citizens banded together to raise $300,000 to build the Elton Hotel. On May 27, 1905, it officially opened with a gala celebration. The hotel was named for Waterbury industrialist James S. Elton, founder and president of Waterbury Brass Co., and later the American Brass Co. He was also the largest shareholder in the hotel corporation. The hotel was the starting point for what was known as "The Ideal Tour," a car tour for the wealthy through New England. The Elton put Waterbury on the map and led to famous people visiting the area. Among the celebrities were baseball greats, Babe Ruth, Ted Williams; John F. Kennedy, who was elected president two days after giving a speech to a crowd of thousands from the hotel's balcony; writer F. Scott Fitzgerald, who met the woman who inspired the character Daisy in his classic *The Great Gatsby*; Waterbury born actress Rosalind Russell, who was honoring her hometown and held a world premier for one of her movies. "The Girl Rush." She signed the guest register on August 17, 1955, and the following day, the flood of 1955 overtook the city. In the 1970s the hotel was converted from a hotel to an office and apartment building. In the 1980s, Theodore H. Martland, former deputy superintendent of schools for the city, bought the building with a team of investors for $1.2 million. In the 1980s the Elton ballroom was reopened after extensive renovation. The domed ceiling was repainted, a period chandelier hung, pillars rebuilt and decorative etched glass installed. In the late '80s and early '90s The Elton fell on hard times because of a glut of vacant office space and elderly residents leaving for cheaper housing. In June 1993, State health care regulators give approval for the Elton to be converted to an assisted living center for elderly people and an adult day care center. *Courtesy Republican-American archives*

ABOVE: Fitzpatrick's Used Cars at 1660 East Main Street in Waterbury at the corner of Idlewood, circa 1939. *Courtesy Bill Fitzpatrick*

RIGHT: Brooklyn Bakery employees in front of their store, Waterbury, 1930s. *Courtesy Sandra and Phil Jusolavic*

ABOVE: Employees of Huxley Motors in Cheshire, circa 1939. From left: Bob Huxley, unidentified, Burt Huxley, Bill Verner, Ray Huxley. *Courtesy Ray Verner*

LEFT: Charles Lanzieri at the back door of Louise's hot dog stand in Waterbury, operated by Charles, his mother and his aunt, 1939. The hot dog stand, a well-known, seasonal eating establishment, was located at the corner of North Main Street and Lakewood Road, Waterbury. *Courtesy Enrico Lanzieri*

FAR LEFT: At the time of this photograph there were more than 95 grocery stores in Torrington, most of which were small neighborhood shops. However, this era also saw the arrival of chain stores such as First National, pictured here, at 270 Main Street in Torrington, circa 1939. Employees Archie Hinchcliffe and Ken Wootton are posed behind the counter. *Courtesy Torrington Historical Society*

CHAPTER THREE

Local Citizens Drive Industry

*"If you are not big enough to lose,
you are not big enough to win."*

— Walter Reuther, labor leader

When industry was coming of age, it was water that powered New England's mills. But it wasn't the water alone that made Connecticut an industrial powerhouse, it was the innovation and foresight of industrialists. The fact that Waterbury became a major center may be tied more to its citizenry than to location. Waterbury had neither an abundance of natural resources nor was it in a convenient location. It did have water, but in New England that is nothing unusual.

Credit the Chase family, the Benedicts, Holmes, the Porter and Grilley brothers, Leavenworth, Croft and James Scovill, the Haydens and Coes and many others for their ingenuity in developing industry up and down the Naugatuck Valley. Their methods and innovations in product development provided jobs that would eventually employ thousands, not only in their shops, but through the ripple of suppliers and merchants.

Although Waterbury is known as the Brass City, it was also a center for timing devices. During the 19th century the region was known as

'The Switzerland of America." There was Waterbury Clock, which became Timex, Lux Clock, General Time and Seth Thomas, which all had their time and place. In Winsted, there was William C. Gilbert, whose legacy is the Gilbert School. These operations, except for Timex, no longer have a presence in the region, but their impact on the Valley remains with the names of many streets and buildings carrying their names.

Meanwhile in New Haven, Charles Goodyear, who invented vulcanized rubber, was looking for a place to use his process and selected Naugatuck to build a small mill because of the abundance of water power. That mill eventually led to U.S. Rubber, which eventually became Uniroyal.

LEFT: Interior of Chase Brass & Copper Co., Thomaston Avenue, Waterville section, circa 1920. *Courtesy Republican-American archives*

RIGHT: Diamond Bottling Works employees, August 12, 1922. This company, later known as Diamond Ginger Ale, Inc., was located on South Main Street in Waterbury. *Courtesy Republican-American archives*

ABOVE: The Rayon Mills strike in Watertown, circa 1933.
Courtesy Republican-American archives

LEFT: Workers at the Scovill Manufacturing Co. factory, Watertown, circa 1930. *Courtesy Republican-American archives*

FAR LEFT: Scovill's tack capping machines, circa 1930. This is part of the equipment which turned out over 1,128,000 buttons and over 450,000 fasteners each working day. *Courtesy Republican-American archives*

ABOVE: Dominic Kowaleski, left, and William Batick cutting ice on Johnson's Pond, Thomaston, 1930s. *Courtesy Republican-American archives*

RIGHT: American Brass Co. locomotive, Waterbury, 1930s. *Courtesy Republican-American archives*

BELOW: Peter Paul plant, Naugatuck, 1930s. *Courtesy Republican-American archives*

FAR RIGHT: A deteriorating saw mill on Bullet Hill Brook, South Britain, Southbury, 1936. *Courtesy Republican-American archives*

LEFT: Waterbury Clock Co. employees on strike, March 1937. *Courtesy Republican-American archives*

RIGHT: Waterbury Clock Co. strike, 1937. *Courtesy Republican-American archives*

ABOVE: Lux Clock factory employees leave work at the end of their shift on Johnson Street, Waterbury, July 31, 1936. The business was founded on East Farm Street in 1917. *Courtesy Republican-American archives*

RIGHT: American Brass Co. employees on strike, April 1, 1938. *Courtesy Republican-American archives*

LEFT: Employees of Heminway & Bartlet Manufacturing in the tubing department, Watertown, 1939. *Courtesy Watertown Historical Society*

ABOVE: Employees of Heminway & Bartlet Manufacturing guide the silk through the braiding machines, Watertown, 1939.
Courtesy Watertown Historical Society

RIGHT: New England Watch Factory in disrepair, corner of South Main and Dover streets, Waterbury, April 1938. *Courtesy Republican-American archives*

CHAPTER FOUR

Schools & Education

"The true teacher defends his pupils against his own personal influence. He inspires self-distrust. He guides their eyes from himself to the spirit that quickens him. He will have no disciple."

— Amos Bronson Alcott, Wolcott native

Education in the first half of the 20th century bears little resemblance to what exists today: no campuses, no labs, few libraries and 50 children in a classroom was not unusual. Still they learned.

This was a time when the one-room school house was slowly drifting toward extinction. Still the Waterbury classrooms of the '30s and '40s were tucked in high-density neighborhoods. Kids walked to school. Even in rural areas, children would walk miles to school. With the coming of school buses, larger, centrally located buildings could be built because children could now ride.

The teachers were women and mostly unmarried. Only at the high school level were students likely to encounter a male teacher.

For many, a grammar school education was all that was required for a place in the work force. Few went to high school and fewer still attended college. In those times, especially on the farms, children were a source of free labor. In the cities, they could work in the factories in their early teens. And for many, that's where they remained the rest of their lives.

These were simpler times, where not a lot of formal training was required to make one's way in life. What knowledge was needed in the workplace was usually learned on the job, while on the farm, it was parental teaching.

However, there still were those who achieved great things. People like Judge John J. Sirica, actor Bob Crane, baseball player Jimmy Piersall, actress Rosalind Russell were all products of Waterbury schools in the first half of the 20th century. And there were countless other lesser-known achievers, such as actresses Jean Dixon and Shirley Grey, sportswriter Dan Parker, all known nationally during their time. Naugatuck produced Adrian, a top Hollywood fashion designer in the '30s and '40s.

LEFT: Students are taught how to draw at the Waterbury Art School in October 1935. The school, located at 111 Grand Street, was started in the mid-1920s. *Courtesy Republican-American archives*

RIGHT: Musical production at St. Joseph School Hall, Waterbury, circa 1925. *Courtesy Mary Ann Larriviere*

LEFT: Mitchell School faculty and students, Woodbury, 1923. *Courtesy Woodbury Public Library*

BELOW: High School graduation class in Watertown, 1924. The high school was housed on the second floor of Baldwin School. First row: Margaret Farrell, Joseph Osborn, Evelyn Quick, Wilfred Farrell, Evelyn Besancon, Robert Allyn, Caroline Northrop. Second row: Arthur Francis, Ada Hunt, Emma Wollenhaupt, Mary Hanning, Dorothy Blanner, Catherine Dwyer, Marie Atwood, Gerald Miller. Third row: Lydia Cake, Marion Dews, Anna Young, Jessie Deavenworth, Paul Johnson, Mildred Towle, Doris Dimock, Gertrude Ransom. *Courtesy Watertown Historical Society*

ABOVE: East Street School, Southington, 1922. Those identified are: last row, boy with the tie over his shoulder as Anthony Renkun. Last row, second boy from left as Chester Renkun. First row, girl with the dog as Helen Renkun. First row, first girl on the right as Mildred Renkun. The dog used to go to school all day. *Courtesy Richard Renkun*

ABOVE: Waterbury Catholic High School graduation, circa 1930.
Courtesy Agnes Rodgers

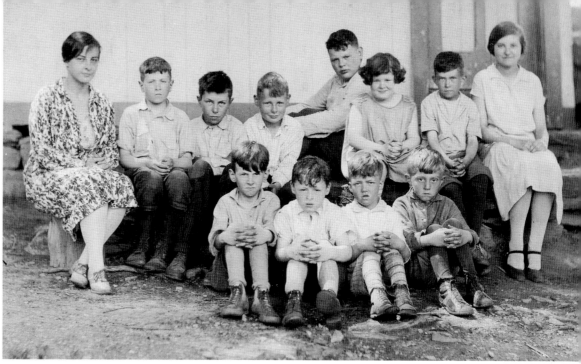

ABOVE: Pierce Hollow District School, Southbury, circa 1929. Pictured, back row: Mrs. Julia Schielke, Harry Lautenschlager, William Lautenschlager, Willis Platt, Edward Platt, Louis Platt, Robert Lautenschlager, Beatrice Lautenschlager. Front row: Townsend Haxwhurst, Leroy Platt, James Miller, I. Smith.
Courtesy Woodbury Public Library

LEFT: Bethlehem school house, 1920s.
Courtesy Republican-American archives

ABOVE: Union City School teachers, circa 1895. In the photos: Helen Prindle, John Fitzpatrick, Iva Callender, Anna Abell, Jane Twitchell, Nellie Brennan, Clara Wood, Belle Meramble. *Courtesy Naugatuck Historical Society*

RIGHT: Kingsbury School, Waterbury, children choose up sides during recess, March 1935. *Courtesy Republican-American archives*

ABOVE: Woodbury High School graduating class of 1933. *Courtesy Woodbury Public Library*

RIGHT: Crosby High School state football champions, 1930. Included in the photo: Mulligan, Dunn, E. DiNapoli, Finkenzeller, Martone, Phelan, Moran, Colby, Burke, Kern, McGrath, Herr, Fryer, Trotta, Yurgaitis, Murphy, Daly, Wilson, M. DiNapoli, Gannutz, Festa, Cronin, Casertano, Eagan, Conlon, Goemey, Sullivan, Smith, J. Murphy, Rompre, and Fitzgerald. *Courtesy Republican-American archives*

LEFT: The old Academy in Salisbury, July 1936. *Courtesy Republican-American archives*

FAR LEFT: Russell School, eighth grade students, 1930s. *Courtesy Dora Whitright*

ABOVE: South School students leaving school for the day, Oakville, September 1935. *Courtesy Republican-American archives*

RIGHT: Watertown's Union Congregational Church Sunday School students, teachers and pastor, 1930s. The Rev. Oscar Locke was the pastor of this church located on Main Street. He is pictured in the back row wearing glasses. *Courtesy Watertown Historical Society*

ABOVE: The Old Academy in Fairfield, 1939. It was built in 1804. *Courtesy Republican-American archives*

LEFT: A crowd watches the Junior Republic boys practice their drills in Litchfield, June 1936.
Courtesy Republican-American archives

BELOW: St. Peter & Paul School eighth grade graduation in 1939, Waterbury. *Courtesy Ruth Farrell Barton*

CHAPTER FIVE

Diversity Shapes Neighborhoods

*"Life is a banquet, and most poor suckers
are starving to death!"*

— Rosalind Russell, Waterbury native in "Auntie Mame," 1958

The 20 years before World War II was both a period of prosperity and a period of want.

In the boom years, the abundance of jobs drew thousands to the region, but when the stock market crashed in 1929, prosperity quickly turned to misery. Fortunately, Waterbury people who could help, did. Agencies were set up locally to do what the federal government could not. Finally toward the end of the '30s, people were back on their feet and when war broke out, there weren't enough of them to fill the demand for labor, especially with the able-bodied young men marching off to war.

The Waterbury of the '20s and '30s was a place of ethnic neighborhoods, each with its own social clubs, churches and retailers. They were something like small towns incorporated into a larger city. The Irish were in the Abrigador and Washington Hill areas, the Lithuanians in Brooklyn, the Italians in the North End and Town Plot, the Polish in the North End and the French in the South End. Most Waterburians lived within two or three miles of downtown. Outlying areas such as Highland Avenue, Bucks Hill and the far East End were still rural.

Larger ethnic groups built churches in their neighborhoods. Many of the present-day Catholic churches were built during the 1920s, most with an accompanying parochial school.

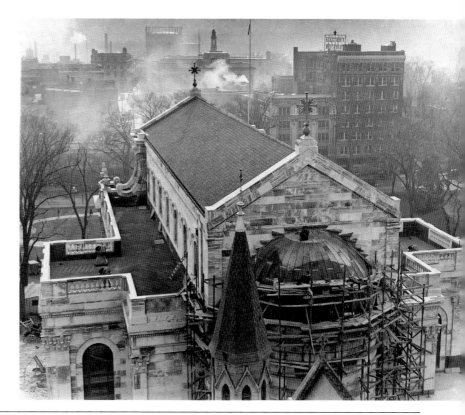

LEFT: Local youngsters woodworking at a YMCA camp in the area, 1933. *Courtesy Republican-American archives*

RIGHT: Construction work on the Immaculate Conception Church at West Main and Prospect streets in Waterbury, circa 1927. *Courtesy Republican-American archives*

ABOVE: This group of Masons poses for the photograph all dressed up in their costumes, 1920s. Frequently the Masons would have plays and perform for the community in the Mason Hall on West Main Street. *Courtesy Dora Whitright*

RIGHT: First Congregational Church, Southington, circa 1920. Notice the two men waving from the top of the spire. *Courtesy Ron Gagliardi*

BELOW: Rod and Gun Club, Thomaston, circa 1925. *Courtesy Republican-American archives*

RIGHT: Litchfield Congregational Church on the Green, circa 1930.
Courtesy Republican-American archives

FAR RIGHT: The Most Rev. John J. Nilan (wearing miter at right), Archbishop of Hartford, blessed the cornerstone at the $1-million Church of the Immaculate Conception being built at West Main and Prospect streets, Waterbury, August 15, 1926.
Courtesy Republican-American archives

ABOVE: St. Paul's Church, Woodbury, circa 1925.
Courtesy Republican-American archives

LEFT: Captain Hurworthy and Captain Lucas pose in front of the Diocese of Connecticut, an Army Mission van, circa 1929. *Courtesy Republican-American archives*

ABOVE: Children work on crafts at the Pearl Street Neighborhood House, Waterbury, July 1931. *Courtesy Republican-American archives*

RIGHT: First contigent of Waterbury young men to leave for Civilian Conservation Corps during the Depression on April 25, 1933. They were photographed outside the Mutual Aid Office on Field Street. Included in this group are: Frank Sortino, Roland Tourangeau, Thomas Hurley, Charles Marchand, Leo Dionne, Edward Nault, Richard H. Lawlor, Bronis Melesky, Laurence Wright, John Ginishus, Frank Lombardo, Nicholas Sullivan, Joseph Strakauskas, Louis Raimo, Angelo Sgrillo, John J. Foley, Biagio Tuccillo and Edward H. Byron. These men were between 19 and 25 years old. *Courtesy Republican-American archives*

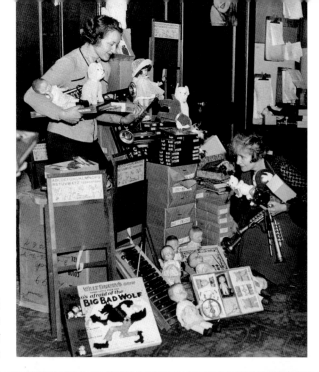

RIGHT: Toy drive for the annual Christmas party sponsored by State Theatre in Waterbury, December 1935. *Courtesy Republican-American archives*

ABOVE: Officers of the state chapter of the DAR attending a meeting at the First Baptist Church, Waterbury, 1936. Pictured left to right, first row: Mrs. John Laidlaw Buel, Mrs. George Maynard Minor, Miss Emeline Street, state regent; Mrs. Frederick P. Latimer, vice regent; and Mrs. J. Laurence Raymond. Second row: Mrs. Charles Gildersleeve, member of the state council, Mrs. William LaPlace, Mrs. Robert S. Walker, regent of Melicent Porter chapter. Third row: Mrs. Phineas Ingalls, a member of the state council; Miss Katherine Matthies, Mrs. Edward Ingraham, Mrs. Henry B. Armstrong, Jr., and Mrs. Howard S. Parsons, recording secretary. *Courtesy Republican-American archives*

LEFT: Garment workers strike, July 24, 1935.
Courtesy Republican-American archives

RIGHT: Newly elected officers of Waterbury's Washington Park Community Club, installed January 1936. Pictured from left to right, seated: James Gladney, recording secretary; Frank Sturges, vice-president; Ramond Grady, president; Albert Lawlor, financial secretary. Standing: Joseph Mulcunry, auditor; Mrs. Michael Kelley, director; Mrs. Mary Blake, auditor; and John Dalton, treasurer.
Courtesy Republican-American archives

ABOVE: Construction work on Middlebury's Congregational Church in 1936. Fire destroyed the previous building as well as Middlebury's town hall on April 8, 1935. *Courtesy Republican-American archives*

LEFT: New slate of Daughters of Italy installed, January 1936. Those known, first row: Miss Olga Piola, Mrs. Samuel Pinto, Mrs. Joseph Parziale, Mrs. Joseph Lombard, Mrs. Ludwig Carosella. Second row: Miss Dolores Paoloni, Miss Louise Mazzaferro, Mrs. Danile Suozzo, Mrs. James D'Andrea. Third row: Miss Lena Macini, Mrs. Mary Ricci, Mrs. Frank Ciampi, Miss Petricone, Mrs. Margaret Spagnuolo. *Courtesy Republican-American archives*

ABOVE: Officers of Waterbury Lodge of Moose installed by several members of the New Haven lodge, April 1936. The members are, front row: William Daley, past dictator; Harry Hubert, dictator; Seth W. Booth, vice-dictator; Henry Carislo, prelate; E.F. Dahl, secretary. Back row: F.J. Egan, treasurer; Patrick Tulley, past dictator; Edgar Harder, trustee; John M. Hannon, past dictator; Henry Baribault, past dictator; Thomas Murphy, trustee, Frank Sturges, inside guard; John Dowling, outside guard. *Courtesy Republican-American archives*

RIGHT: The original organizers of Irish-American Social Club, Waterbury, 1936. Pictured, left to right, first row: John O'Sullivan, Arthur J. Lunny, Edward Loughrain, Michael Fitzmaurice, Frank Keavney, William Fleming. Second row: John Lynch, Martin Sugrue, Thomas Reidy, Robert Stack, Patrict Leen, Michael Lunch, Garrett Casey. The club was formed on July 13, 1934 by a group of men dedicated to be of service to Irish residents during the time when America was in a state of transition. The club grew from 13 members to well over 2,000. *Courtesy Republican-American archives*

TOP RIGHT: St. Thomas Church, Thomaston, February 1936. *Courtesy Republican-American archives*

LEFT & BELOW: Groups from the Lions Club home for underprivileged children visit Woodbury, 1936.
Courtesy Republican-American archives

LEFT: Young boys grab a drink in the town fountain in Salisbury, June 1936.
Courtesy Republican-American archives

RIGHT: St. Joseph's Catholic Church, Winsted, March 1936.
Courtesy Republican-American archives

LEFT: Bullet Hill School, Southbury, 1936. At one time the second floor was used as a town hall. *Courtesy Republican-American archives*

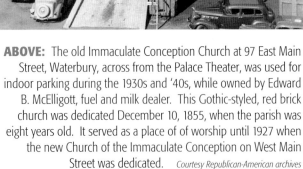

ABOVE: The old Immaculate Conception Church at 97 East Main Street, Waterbury, across from the Palace Theater, was used for indoor parking during the 1930s and '40s, while owned by Edward B. McElligott, fuel and milk dealer. This Gothic-styled, red brick church was dedicated December 10, 1855, when the parish was eight years old. It served as a place of of worship until 1927 when the new Church of the Immaculate Conception on West Main Street was dedicated. *Courtesy Republican-American archives*

RIGHT: Waterbury WPA band, December 1938. The WPA was a work relief program created during the Roosevelt presidency to help the unemployed. *Courtesy Republican-American archives*

ABOVE: Interior of the Waterbury Elks Lodge, October 1938. *Courtesy Republican-American archives*

ABOVE: Unemployment compensation is handed out in Waterbury, January 3, 1938. *Courtesy Republican-American archives*

LEFT: Christ Church, Roxbury, circa 1939. *Courtesy Republican-American archives*

ABOVE: Construction of St. Anthony's Catholic Church, Prospect, circa 1939.
Courtesy Republican-American archives

LEFT: Children show off treats they found during an Easter egg hunt in Platts Mills, Waterbury, April 1938. *Courtesy Republican-American archives*

CHAPTER SIX
Recreation Takes Many Forms

"Oh, we got trouble
Right here in the Brass City
Right here in the Brass City
With a capital "T" and that rhymes with "P" and that stands for pool,
That stands for pool.
We sure got trouble. We sure got trouble
right here in the Brass City, right here."

— advertisement for the opening of the Wooster Billiard Parlor on East Main Street, Waterbury

Exercise equipment in the old days was a baseball bat and a glove.

Waterbury's parks were among the best around and citizens put them to good use. Fulton Park was designed by Frederick Olmsted, the same fellow who laid out Central Park in New York. Waterbury's other major parks were Hamilton Park and later Municipal Stadium. For many a youngster, however, a park was often an empty lot.

From these litter-strewn sandlots, however, came a few who went on to bigger things. Johnny Moore, from the Waterville section, was a lifetime .307 hitter in 10 big league seasons in the '30s. Jimmy Piersall played 17 years in the majors. There were others of lesser stature who also had a cup of coffee in the majors. Waterbury's Roger Conner is

considered the Major Leagues' first home run slugger. It was he who would be eclipsed by Babe Ruth.

Those also were the days of the City Amateur League in Waterbury where thousands would watch local young men play baseball. Sunday leagues populated many of the smaller towns as well.

Waterbury also had a championship fight, and there was golf at a country club, basketball at the Armory and high school athletics, which in those days often saw crowds of 2,000 fans and up.

Aside from athletics, there was always the movies, restaurants and amusements. A big day was when the circus came to town. Tents were pitched, usually on West Main Street and Thomaston Avenue in Waterbury and on Park Avenue in Torrington.

Sunday was a day to relax after church because stores were not allowed to open, factories were closed and there was no TV. It made for family time — a day at Lake Quassapuag in Middlebury or Savin Rock in West Haven, or simply a walk in the woods or a swim in one of the many area ponds.

LEFT: Young and the young at heart visited the circus when it came through Waterbury in the 1930s. *Courtesy Republican-American archives*

RIGHT: Crowd of local children wait for their name to be drawn for the jar of candy at the Easter egg hunt at Hamilton Park, 1928. *Courtesy Republican-American archives*

ABOVE: An event held in the lobby of Colonial Trust Co., located on West Main Street in Waterbury, circa 1920. *Courtesy Mattatuck Museum*

TOP RIGHT: Scovill soccer team, early 1920's. The manager in the back row in a suit is identified as Jose Bandeira; next to him, on right, Manuel Simoes; middle row, first on right, John Freire; back row, first on left, "Scottie." *Courtesy Jack and Gloria Correia*

RIGHT: Naugatuck's Mohawk football team, 1920. Front row: Jimmie Pettit, Joe Shanley, Alex Schmitz, _____Reynolds, and Mike Reynolds. Second row: Otto Hermanot, Jake Mariano, Vince Reynolds, Joe Rodits and Dave Walsh. Third row: Louie Lengyel, Alex Sullivan, Joe Darabus, Florence Sullivan. Back row: Tony Mariano and Howard Humphries. Standing, left to right, Ed Kenney, Charlie Walsh and Jim Cuddy (coach). This team had four sets of brothers. *Courtesy Naugatuck Historical Society*

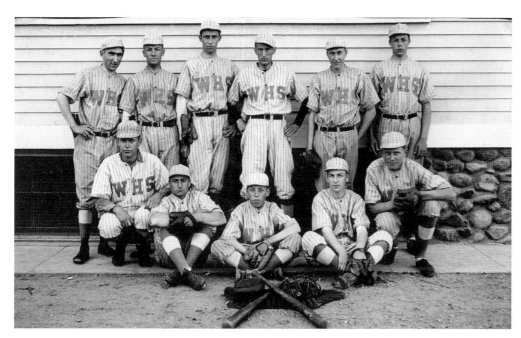

ABOVE: Woodbury High School baseball team, 1923. Pictured, left to right, back row: Frank O'Brien, Minor Cartwright, Fred Perry, George Cahill, Frank Strong, Robert Crane. Front row: James Tomlinson, Oscar Warner, Herbert Fowler, Earl Eyre, William Wenzel. *Courtesy Woodbury Public Library*

RIGHT: St. Francis Xavier School baseball team, Waterbury, 1923. Pictured are, W. Bowen, H. Meaney, G.V. Losey, Father James Butler, H. Thompson, S. Fitzgibbons, Joe Wall. Standing: J. Slattery, J. Cavanaugh, C. Klobedanz, H. Bowen, Ed Curley, W. Reilley, Dr. Ed Kemp, J. Walsh, T. Keane, J. Dunn, T. Purcell, Tom Byrnes. Mascots in the front are unidentified. *Courtesy Republican-American archives*

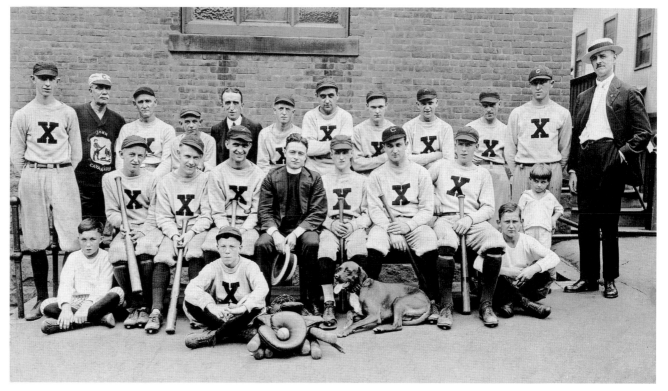

ABOVE & FAR RIGHT: Crowd lines up in front of The Waterbury Republican office on Grand Street to watch the World Series on the play board, October 1925. *Courtesy Republican-American archives*

RIGHT: Ice skating at Fulton Park, Waterbury, 1920s. *Courtesy Republican-American archives*

Recreation Takes Many Forms

LEFT: This large crowd is gathered on Water Street in Torrington to hear the results of a Torrington High School basketball game that was being held in Chicago. As the top team in the state, the 1925 team, known as the "Wonder Five," earned the right to compete in the national tournament. With the aid of a reporter, details of the tournament games were transmitted via telegraph from Chicago to Torrington. Torrington was eliminated in the third round after losing 35-14 to a team from Wheeler, Miss.
Courtesy Torrington Historical Society

ABOVE: Crowds gather in front of this playograph in front of the Waterbury Democrat in hopes to "watch" the World Series in Waterbury, October 1926. *Courtesy Republican-American archives*

RIGHT: Production crew of a movie made in Waterbury, 1928. They are standing in front of the Waterbury Republican office. Notice the latest news is posted on signs behind the crew. Breaking news was the following: high school boys in court today; man fined $100 for drunken driving; Britain sends ship of war to near east; French debt offer rejected by U.S. *Courtesy Republican-American archives*

Recreation Takes Many Forms

ABOVE: A crowd of 4,000 people attended the Republican-American Silver Skates Derby at Hamilton Park, January 26, 1929. *Courtesy Republican-American archives*

ABOVE: Children of all ages enjoyed the circus when it came through Waterbury in 1928. *Courtesy Republican-American archives*

RIGHT: Local residents enjoy an afternoon at the circus when it came to town in 1929. *Courtesy Republican-American archives*

TOP: The Republican and American sponsored a flying contest, 1929.
Courtesy Republican-American archives

ABOVE: Washington Hills Athletic Club, circa 1929. *Courtesy Patricia/Ned Mencio*

RIGHT: St. Francis Cadets baseball team in the late 1920s. *Courtesy Patricia/Ned Mencio*

Recreation Takes Many Forms

ABOVE: The Republican and American sponsored a cooking class in Waterbury, September 1930. *Courtesy Republican-American archives*

RIGHT: Members of the Watertown Hunt Club, November 23, 1930.
Courtesy Republican-American archives

ABOVE: Lobby of the State Theatre, Waterbury, 1930s. *Courtesy Republican-American archives*

LEFT: Peg Sugdinis is diving as the photographer takes the photo of her and the other swimmers at Chase Park, 1930. *Courtesy Republican-American archives*

RIGHT: Ice skaters enjoy an afternoon on the frozen pond at Fulton Park, Waterbury circa 1931.
Courtesy Republican-American archives

ABOVE: St. Joseph's School basketball team, 1930. *Courtesy Knights of Lithuania*

LEFT: Knights of Lithuania girls gymnastics team, circa 1930.
Courtesy Knights of Lithuania

Recreation Takes Many Forms

RIGHT: Ice skating at Hamilton Park, 1933. *Courtesy Republican-American archives*

ABOVE: These hunters display their catch of the day, November 1933. *Courtesy Republican-American archives*

LEFT: Girl Scouts cool off in Bantam Lake in 1930. *Courtesy Republican-American archives*

ABOVE: Fresh Air Children experience horseback rides in the Watertown area, July 1932. *Courtesy Republican-American archives*

LEFT: Men spend a relaxing afternoon in the lobby of the YMCA, February 1935. In the distance a newspaper headline reads: Soviet Russia Today - Hearst Lies About Soviet Union. The banner on the back wall says Inter-Club Hand Ball Champions, 1933. The banner on the right wall says Kenoshas Inter Club-Track Champions 1934. *Courtesy Republican-American archives*

FAR LEFT: Children from New York came to the Waterbury area as part of the "Fresh Air Children's" program, July 14, 1932. This was a program to get the city kids out to experience life in the country. *Courtesy Republican-American archives*

ABOVE: Waterbury children at the Brooklyn and Town Plot playground, Waterbury, July 1935. *Courtesy Republican-American archives*

RIGHT: Sisters, Dora (left), and Ellen Eurell before finals of a tennis match at Chase Park, Waterbury, 1936. Dora would beat her older sister in this match. *Courtesy Dora Whitright*

FAR RIGHT: Naugatuck, girls basketball team 1936. Included in the photo: B. Paplauskas, Ethel Kovach, Helen Patterson, Eleanor O'Shea, Alice Schilgan, Alice Dolan, Mary Moore, Margaret Chittenden. *Courtesy Naugatuck Historical Society*

LEFT: Participants are off for the start of the first annual Soap Box Derby, sponsored by the Republican-American, July 19, 1936. Pictured, from left to right: Roland Hamel, Russell Schmitt, Albert Forgue, Gustave Luschenat. The race started at East Main Street, from Calvary Cemetery to Mattatuck Mfg. Co. *Courtesy Republican-American archives*

BELOW: And they're off… Soap Box Derby participants during the start of the race at East Main Street from Calvary Cemetery to Mattatuck Mfg. Co., July 19, 1936. The derby, sponsored by the Republican-American, was a popular event in Waterbury. *Courtesy Republican-American archives*

BOTTOM LEFT: Robert Rowley was the winner at the Soap Box Derby sponsored by the Republican-American, July 19, 1936.
Courtesy Republican-American archives

LEFT: Opening day at Chase Country Club, Wolcott, June 26, 1937. Chase officials were among those to first tee off on the rolling course. Pictured, from left: F.S. Chase, F.A. Jackle, C.E. Hart, W.C. Husted, J.J. Gilbert and Bud Geoghegan, Highland Country Club professional.
Courtesy Republican-American archives

RIGHT: John Uniakas, and Anthony Bogush are shown with the six fish they caught at Lake Waramaug in January 1936. One of the fish was a seven-pound pickerel which measured 27" long. *Courtesy Republican-American archives*

ABOVE: Local Girl Scouts practice archery skills in 1937.
Courtesy Republican-American archives

LEFT: Local hunters display their catch of the day, 1937. Pictured, from left: Sam Fenn (?), Chas Champagne, Paul Johnson, Louis Davidson. *Courtesy Republican-American archives*

ABOVE: Ringling Bros., Barnum & Bailey Circus side-shows drew lots of people in Waterbury, 1930s. *Courtesy Republican-American archives*

RIGHT: Warriors A.C. sports team, circa 1939. Some of these men would lose their lives serving in the United States military during World War II. *Courtesy Anthony Santoro*

FAR RIGHT: Children sledding after a snow storm in Woodbury, 1938. They are identified as Thomas Phillips, Franklin Murphy, Clarence Shean Jr., Thomas Crownshaw, William Fleming, Randall Barnes, Allfred Platt, Millicent Shean, Nancy Shean, Irene Fleming, Claire Fleming and Marion Platt. *Courtesy Republican-American archives*

Recreation Takes Many Forms

CHAPTER SEVEN

Automobile Brings Change

"I will build a car for the great multitude. It will be large enough for the family, but small enough for the individual to run and care for. It will be low in price so that no man making a good salary will be unable to own one--and enjoy with his family the blessing of hours of pleasure in God's great open spaces."

— Henry Ford

These days, people think of the Internet as the great society-changing advance in technology. It has forever altered the way we do research, the way we write letters, the way we learn about the world. In the early 20th century, the change agent was the automobile.

Rural Litchfield County was a patchwork of small farming communities with isolated pockets of manufacturing in places like Torrington, New Milford, Litchfield and the Winsted district of Winchester. Townsfolk simply didn't travel.

The valley towns along the Naugatuck River were humming with industry and they were stitched together largely with street car and rail lines. People walked and drove carriages. Until the automobile.

Now, Northwestern Connecticut is laced with highways; some, called super highways, allow motorists to rocket nonstop from Winsted to Bridgeport at speeds averaging 70 mph—almost unimaginable at the turn of the last century. Waterbury's mix-master interchange carries drivers on three levels and the Interstate virtually wiped out whole neighborhoods in the name of travel.

With motorized transportation came trucks and buses, vehicles that would undo much of the prosperity the railroads had brought to the Northwest Corner. The great train stations of Waterbury, New Haven and Hartford still stand. North Canaan, badly damaged by fire, will be rebuilt. Naugatuck's train station has become a museum and office space. Thomaston's is a rail museum and traditionalists hope the Torrington station will be reborn as part of that city's downtown makeover.

For city folks, the automobile meant trips to the countryside on weekends and the beginning of suburbia, the small towns where the majority of Connecticut's population now resides.

LEFT: A Hartford passenger train pulled by engine No. 1004 clears the Terryville Tunnel, circa 1931. C.L. "Mort" Mortison, The Republican's long time cartoonist is on the bank above the engine. *Courtesy Republican-American archives*

RIGHT: Mr. Molby (Molby Garage), and his passengers enjoy a ride in a Pierce Arrow, circa 1920. *Courtesy Republican-American archives*

ABOVE: Last run of the trolley between Winsted and Torrington, January 5, 1929. Staff members, from left are, Cortland Horton, William Shay, Edward Healy, Grover Roys, Leon Dayfield, Baptist Zlecken, Miles Rood, John Abatta, B. Pars and Joseph Rowinski. *Courtesy Republican-American archives*

ABOVE: Bethany Air Service hangar at Bethany Airport, circa 1929. The airport was an important stop for planes flying between New York and Boston. *Courtesy Republican-American archives*

RIGHT: Tearing up the trolley lines in Woodbury, circa 1930. *Courtesy Republican-American archives*

Automobile Brings Change

LEFT: Last of the Woodbury line at Canfield Corner, October 1930.
Courtesy Republican-American archives

ABOVE: The New Hampshire Railroad, "The Comet" drew crowds of people to the railroad station in Waterbury, May 1935. The Comet was a flash boiler (Stanley Steamer). *Courtesy Republican-American archives*

RIGHT: An early garbage truck in Waterbury, April 1934. *Courtesy Republican-American archives*

ABOVE: The first trolley to cross the new Washington Avenue Bridge on South Main Street led two others in a final salute to electric passenger transportation between Waterbury and points south. Buses were the transportation of the day between Waterbury and Naugatuck. Those in the picture include: Otis Fairley, motorman; A.B. Foster, roadmaster for the Connecticut Co.; Herbert Scott-Smith, bridge construction engineer; City Engineer Cairus, Assistant City Engineer, Charles Root, and Patsy Capello, Connecticut Co. foreman, and C. Marrabattini, an additional foreman for the trolley company.
Courtesy Republican-American archives

LEFT: The last trolley in Waterbury ran on May 24, 1937, between Waterbury and Watertown. The motorman is William McGee.
Courtesy Republican-American archives

RIGHT: Railroad crossing near the Naugatuck River, Thomaston, 1930s. *Courtesy Republican-American archives*

TOP RIGHT: Last trolley between Watertown and Waterbury, May 1937. *Courtesy Republican-American archives*

CHAPTER EIGHT

Need for Public Services Grows

"You have powers you never dreamed of. You can do things you never thought you could do. There are no limitations in what you can do except the limitations of your own mind."

— Darwin P. Kingsley, business executive

"Common sense is the knack of seeing things as they are, and doing things as they ought to be done."

— Harriet Beecher Stowe, Litchfield native

The period between the two world wars brought changes never before seen in such a short period. Whole slices of Northwest Connecticut were becoming urbanized. The factory towns along the Naugatuck River promised steady wages and regular work hours drawing people away from the farms. Add in the huge number of Europeans arriving into the river towns daily, and it was obvious there would be a greater need for services.

With urbanization, came the need for police, firefighters, public works and health service workers. Government on all levels began to make greater intrusions into neighborhood life.

The dirt roads of the horse and buggy days gave way to paved roads for the automobile. They had to be maintained. Schools had to be built. Bigger buildings and factories meant more firefighters and better equipment. The Great Depression, Prohibition and population growth spurred the need for more police.

With these services, came taxes, something with which a farm society had little acquaintance. Life was becoming more complicated. Though most people were still pretty self-reliant, times were changing.

The Great Depression did bring forth many public works projects, many of which exist today. Roads, post offices, recreational areas all benefited from government programs meant to bring work to the unemployed.

LEFT: Waterbury Police Department patrol wagon, 1931. *Courtesy Republican-American archives*

RIGHT: Woodbury fire engine, with Fire Chief Frank E. Tuttle standing and Chief Engineer Fred St. Pierre at the wheel. This was Woodbury's first fire engine. *Courtesy Woodbury Public Library*

ABOVE: Litchfield County Courthouse in Litchfield, circa 1925.
Courtesy Republican-American archives

TOP RIGHT: Charlotte Hungerford Hospital, Torrington, circa 1930.
Courtesy Republican-American archives

RIGHT: Newton Town Hall, circa 1929. *Courtesy Republican-American archives*

Need for Public Services Grows

ABOVE: Waterbury National Guardsmen practice maneuvers in 1931.
Courtesy Republican-American archives

LEFT: Woodbury Fire Deparment, circa 1931.   *Courtesy Woodbury Public Library*

BELOW: Waterbury Police Department cars, 1931.   *Courtesy Republican-American archives*

RIGHT: A GAR gathering to honor five Civil War Veterans, February 1932. *Courtesy Republican-American archives*

ABOVE: Patients in the waiting area at Saint Mary's Hospital clinic, Waterbury, February 1931. *Courtesy Republican-American archives*

LEFT: Waterbury Post Office workers sort the piles of Christmas gifts during the 1931 holiday season. *Courtesy Republican-American archives*

Need for Public Services Grows

ABOVE: Firehouse in Bantam, 1930s. *Courtesy Republican-American archives*

RIGHT: Members of the Naugatuck Fire Department, 1935.
Courtesy Naugatuck Historical Society

ABOVE: Charles A. Babin, Waterbury Postmaster, 1935.
Courtesy Republican-American archives

LEFT: Crowd gathers for the laying of the cornerstone for the U.S. Post Office on Grand Street in Waterbury, May 1932. *Courtesy Republican-American archives*

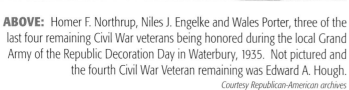

ABOVE: Homer F. Northrup, Niles J. Engelke and Wales Porter, three of the last four remaining Civil War veterans being honored during the local Grand Army of the Republic Decoration Day in Waterbury, 1935. Not pictured and the fourth Civil War Veteran remaining was Edward A. Hough.
Courtesy Republican-American archives

RIGHT: Homer Northrup, Civil War veteran, speaking at Memorial Day exercises in front of the honor roll at Library Park, Waterbury, May 1935. Northrup was one of the four remaining Civil War veterans in the Waterbury area. *Courtesy Republican-American archives*

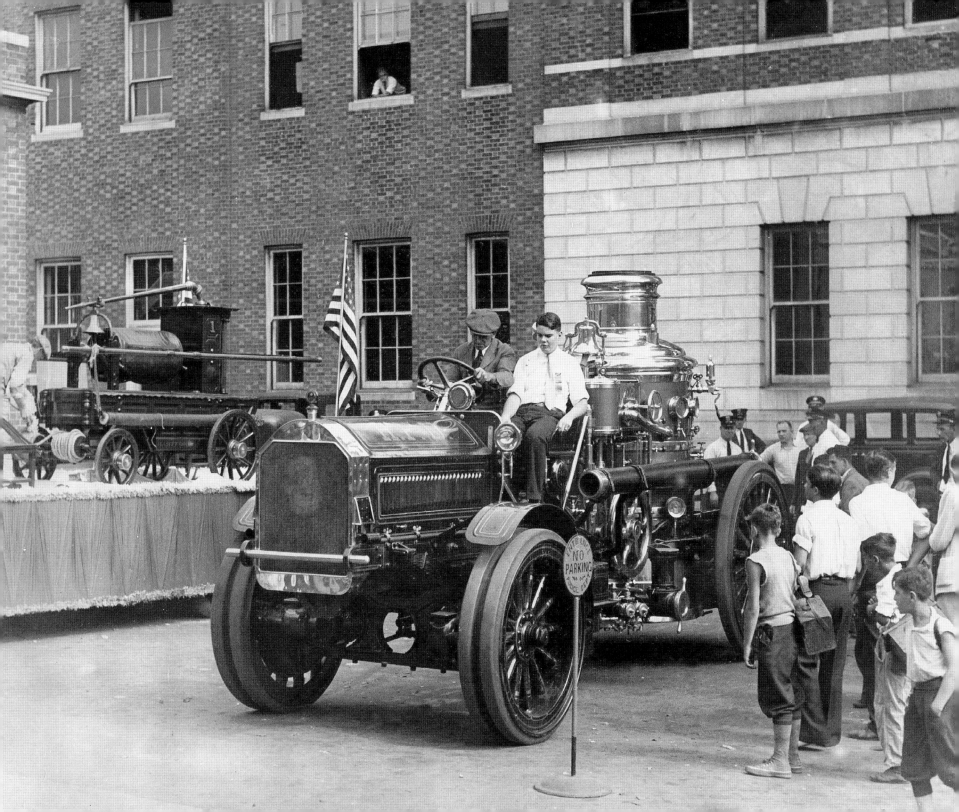

LEFT: Hamden Town Hall, 1930s. *Courtesy Republican-American archives*

ABOVE: Connecticut's Tercentennary Celebration activities at the Soldiers Monument, Winsted, September 1935. *Courtesy Republican-American archives*

RIGHT: Children read books at the Brooklyn Library in the 1930s. The library appears to have little or no heat because all the children have their coats on. *Courtesy Republican-American archives*

Need for Public Services Grows

ABOVE: Plymouth Town Hall in Terryville, 1930s. *Courtesy Republican-American archives*

RIGHT: Terryville Fire Station, 1930s. *Courtesy Republican-American archives*

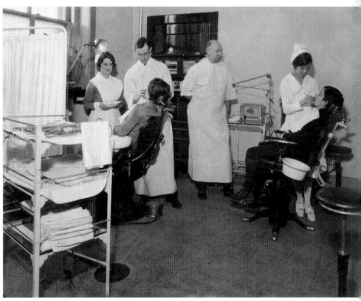

ABOVE: Dental clinic at Saint Mary's Hospital, Waterbury, 1930s. Included in the photo: Dr. Driscoll, dental intern; Dr. Borchardt and Miss Marian Arber, school hygienist. *Courtesy Republican-American archives*

LEFT: Last minute Christmas presents are being sent from the Waterbury Post Office, 1935. *Courtesy Republican-American archives*

LEFT: Company L, National Guard, Torrington, circa 1935.
Courtesy Republican-American archives

RIGHT: National Guard practices drills in Waterbury, August 1935.
Courtesy Republican-American archives

BELOW: The only motorized, volunteer fire department in Waterbury's industrial plants, circa 1936. The company was organized in 1917 when a new truck was purchased. The truck served to bring the men, representing various departments of the Waterville Chase Metal Works plant, to all parts of the company property to fight fires. Daniel M. Sullivan, head of the millwright department, was the chief. He is shown with the driver, Jack Raynor. Others in the photo, from left: Walter O. Horman, Frank Seery, Patrick Shea, George Baker, and Irving Tucker.
Courtesy Republican-American archives

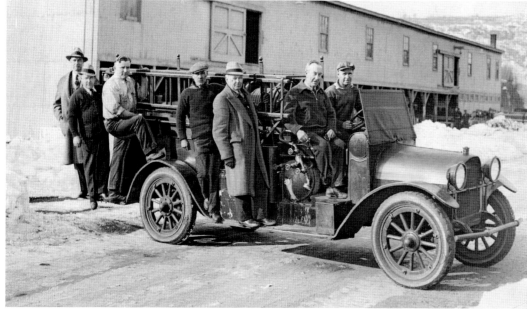

ABOVE: New fire fighting equipment in Roxbury, February 1935. Joseph S. Hartwee is at the wheel and beside him is Walter J. Booth. This photo was taken in front of the Roxbury fire house. *Courtesy Republican-American archives*

ABOVE: A view of the Middlebury Town Hall and Congregational Church after reconstruction following the disastrous fire in 1935. Photo circa 1937. *Courtesy Republican-American archives*

ABOVE: Emptying liquor into the sewer during Prohibition, Waterbury, circa 1930. *Courtesy Republican-American archives*

RIGHT: Road work at Dead Man's Curve, Naugatuck, July 1936. *Courtesy Republican-American archives*

BELOW: U.S. Post Office in Seymour, circa 1936. *Courtesy Republican-American archives*

ABOVE: New England Home for Crippled Children, Newington, March 1937. *Courtesy Republican-American archives*

LEFT: Salisbury Town Hall, June 1936. *Courtesy Republican-American archives*

ABOVE: Waterbury City Hall, 1936. *Courtesy Republican-American archives*

RIGHT: Citizen Engine Co., No. 2 in Seymour, circa 1936. *Courtesy Republican-American archives*

LEFT: First Selectman E.R. Kaiser, Thomaston, is shown as he accepts for the town the monument in honor of Thomaston men who gave their lives in World War I, November 7, 1936. *Courtesy Republican-American archives*

RIGHT: Members of the Hotchkissville Fire Department, circa 1937. Pictured left to right: Ernest Bryant, Alfred Eyer Sr., Ernest Bull, Frank Johnson, Percy Young, Alfred Eyre Jr., Francis Goodwind, Charles Mallette. *Courtesy Woodbury Public Library*

BELOW: Exterior of the U.S. Post Office in Bristol, March 19, 1937. *Courtesy Republican-American archives*

BOTTOM RIGHT: Waterbury Patrolman John McWeeney is shown sending out a message from headquarters, June 1937. *Courtesy Republican-American archives*

ABOVE: A busy Post Office during the 1937 holiday season in Waterbury. *Courtesy Republican-American archives*

RIGHT: Hamilton Park swimming pool was the scene of a National Safety Council accident safety program on July 27, 1937. Standing by the car, from left, are: Edward Roberts, field representative of the safety council; Paul Guglielmo, pool supervisor; motor patrolman Thomas Redding, James Little, of the traffic safety commission; Ralph Ellis, in car, manager of the council; Capt. William Duggan, head of the motor patrol, and Charles McWeeney of the traffic accident prevention squad. *Courtesy Republican-American archives*

BELOW: U.S. Post Office in Thomaston, January 1938. *Courtesy Republican-American archives*

ABOVE: Road work continues as part of the unemployment relief project in downtown Waterbury, 1937. *Courtesy Republican-American archives*

RIGHT: Naugatuck Police Chief John Gormley, June 1939. *Courtesy Republican-American archives*

FAR RIGHT: Patients of the New England Home for Crippled Children in Newington, March 1937. *Courtesy Republican-American archives*

ABOVE: Saint Mary's School of Nursing graduates in 1939. Members of the class, from left, first row: Anna Muha, Candita Palo, Anne Stulginski, Sophie Kawecki, Catherine McVerry, Anne Szymanski, Teresa Pizzuto, Louise Carpenter, Agnes Reilly, Marie Charron, Emma Urgitis, Arline O'Donnell, Genevive Robillard, Jane Cadrain, Esther Sullivan. Second row: Catherine Whalen, Rita Lanoue, Elizabeth Holmes, Isabelle Pastore, Bernice Gudzuinas, Anna Wiblyi; Third row: Sally Slusarcyk, Mary Horan, Dorothy McWeeney, Elizabeth Sayers, Estelle Andrusiewich, Elizabeth Erichetto, Eleanor and Ruth Nalband (twins), Mary Marrone, Jane Judge, Agnes Carragan, Elizabeth Prill, Marie Deconnck, Agnes Carrolan. *Courtesy Republican-American archives*

LEFT: Fairfield Town House, September 26, 1939.
Courtesy Republican-American archives

ABOVE: Jingles Donahue, long-time Waterbury policeman, circa 1939.
Courtesy Republican-American archives

RIGHT: U.S. Post Office at Church and Main streets in Torrington, circa 1939.   *Courtesy Republican-American archives*

LEFT: Waterbury Fire Department demonstrates the abilities of its new hook and ladder truck that arrived by train in 1939. The demonstration took place on Field Street. The two buildings at center and right were designed by Cass Gilbert.

Courtesy Republican-American archives

CHAPTER NINE

Ordinary People Pull Together

"And in the end, it's not the years in your life that count.
It's the life in your years."

— Abraham Lincoln

They were ordinary people, but together they were a force. Asking little but decent food, shelter and better lives for their children, they toiled in Waterbury's factories, turning out products used around the world. Owners prospered.

Seeing afar the lives of the wealthy, the factory worker also sought a share of the rewards. As individuals they were powerless, but in numbers there was strength. With concerns for workplace safety, demands for better pay and more benefits, industrialists now had to deal with labor unions.

It was the common man who went to work, provided for his family and went to church on Sunday. With newly won labor concessions, there was more money pumped into the economy, which likely had a lot to do with ending the Depression.

There was now money for clothes, family life and services that were previously unavailable to most folks.

Times were good once again.

LEFT: Slovak immigrants Michael and Anna Metro with their seven children. Michael and Anna immigrated to the United States in the 1890s, living first in Bridgeport before moving to Torrington. Michael was employed for many years by the Warrenton Woolen Mill and later, by the American Brass Co. The Metros were one of Torrington's many Slovak families who helped establish Sacred Heart Church.   *Courtesy Paul and Roberta Kruppa*

RIGHT: Mrs. Ida N. Munson of Woodbury, February 1936.   *Courtesy Republican-American archives*

ABOVE: Enrico and Louise Lanzieri swimming at Lakewood Park in Waterbury, 1920. *Courtesy Enrico Lanzieri*

RIGHT: George Bennett with son, Austen of Southbury, early 1920s. *Courtesy Lynn Bennett Plourde*

LEFT: Wedding photo of Clifford Farrell and Rose (DuBoise). They are pictured at left. The other couple is unidentified.
Courtesy Francis Barton

RIGHT: Engagement photo of Nancy (DeLeo) Alessio and "Patsy" Alessio, circa 1923. *Courtesy Dan Alessio*

ABOVE: Clem Bronson, ice cream manufacturer in Torrington, circa 1928. He was good friends with his competitor Moses Doyle Jr. *Courtesy Robert Doyle*

LEFT: Out for a snowy ride on Mansion House Road, Southbury, 1920s. Pictured is James Lockwood, left, and Austen Bennett, right. On sled is Reginald Bennett. Kingsland can be seen in the distance.
Courtesy Lynn Bennett Plourde

ABOVE: DeLeo Family photo at what was then 84 Hamden Avenue, Waterbury, circa 1932. Pictured, left to right, back row: Ralphelle DeLeo, Philip Deleo, Rose Bianco. Front row: Rocky Bianco, Grandma, and Linda Bianco. *Courtesy Dan Alessio*

RIGHT: Dan Alessio after his new hair cut from his father, Waterbury, circa 1929. *Courtesy Dan Alessio*

FAR RIGHT: The wedding of Rosalina and Elzear Grenier, Watertown, June 26, 1929. Left to right: Adrien Gelinas, brother of the bride; Rosalina, bride; Elzear, groom; Narcisse Grenier, father of the groom. This couple was married at the old St. John's Church on Main Street, Watertown. *Courtesy Watertown Historical Society*

RIGHT: Moses Wallace Doyle Sr., "Town Farm" superintendent, Litchfield, 1895. "Town Farm" was used for those down and out or those who had difficulty with the law. This photograph, known as "The Country Gentleman," was entered into a contest and won. Doyle was married at the age of 41 and had five children. He also worked for a time in a brass mill.
Courtesy Robert Doyle

ABOVE: Austen A. Bennett with hunting dogs at his family home on Mansion House Road, Southbury, circa 1932. The family raised hunting dogs. His family also purchased, sold and boarded dogs as well. It was called Southbury Kennel. *Courtesy Lynn Bennett Plourde*

LEFT: Friends pose for this photograph at the Bennett home on Mansion House Road, in the White Oak section of Southbury, circa 1936. Left to right: Ed Munson, Reg Bennett, Austen Bennett and Harry Wilson. Austen purchased the 1936 Ford when it was new for $612. Reg Bennett is Austen's younger brother. *Courtesy Lynn Bennett Plourde*

ABOVE: Townsend "Skip" Garrigus and his dog in the front of an old flatbed truck on their property across from the Town Hall in Southbury. *Courtesy Shirley McIlroy*

RIGHT: Agnes Plourde with her son Irving, Waterbury, circa 1939. *Courtesy Virginia Plourde*

TOP RIGHT: A 1937 interview with Mayor Hayes in Waterbury (center, in light suit). To Hayes' left is Ray Fitzpatrick, conducting the interview and Bill Fitzpatrick at far right. *Courtesy Bill Fitzpatrick*

ABOVE: Roger Payne on the milk stand at Sperry's farm on Woodbury Road, Watertown, circa 1939. *Courtesy Roger Payne*

LEFT: The Petro-Roy family in front of A.P. Roy's on the corner of Sperry and West Main streets, Waterbury, circa 1939. *Courtesy Suzanne Maia*

CHAPTER TEN

Weather, Wrecks Take a Toll

*"We must accept finite disappointment,
but never lose infinite hope."*

— Martin Luther King, Jr., civil rights leader

Tragedy is never planned, but its impact can be devastating to thousands and millions or just a few.

In the days between the two world wars, there were no huge disasters such as the fire in 1902 that burned much of downtown Waterbury or the Great Flood of 1955 that did millions in damage from Winsted to Derby.

The hurricane of 1938 did hit the region, but almost all the damage from that storm was along the shore, especially in New London County and in Rhode Island.

The train wrecks frequent in the 19th century became rare because of safety regulations and technological innovations. With far fewer automobiles, there wasn't the accident tally of today. Better firefighting equipment limited fire damage, though there were a few blazes of note.

The greatest threat to Waterburians was the weather. Without the technology of today, reliable predictions using computers, weather satellites and radar, were not possible. Although each year would usually bring at least one crippling storm, the impact was less because most people walked to work. The snow might remain on streets for days because removal equipment was primitive by today's standards. In the country, there were one-horse-open sleighs and snow was packed rather than plowed.

LEFT: Hundreds of spectators gathered at the scene of the Waterbury-Winsted train wreck on January 23, 1929. *Courtesy Republican-American archives*

RIGHT: Union City fire where buildings were completely destroyed, January 1928.
Courtesy Republican-American archives

ABOVE: Flood relief effort at the Gem Theatre to assist vicitims of the 1924 flood in Naugatuck. *Courtesy Naugatuck Historical Society*

LEFT: A view of floodwaters in Naugatuck, April 1924. *Courtesy Naugatuck Historical Society*

ABOVE: Workers clear the roads of snow left behind during the blizzard that hit Waterbury in 1926. *Courtesy Republican-American archives*

RIGHT: The great fire on Maple Street, across from the firehouse in Naugatuck, 1921. It burned out several stores including, Frank Grant Grocery, a confectionary store and Madden's Dry Goods Store. *Courtesy Naugatuck Historical Society*

Weather, Wrecks Take a Toll

ABOVE: All bundled up and puffing a cigar, James J. Dillon of Waterbury was able to travel smoothly on Center Street, Waterbury, February 22, 1934, following a blizzard that paralyzed motor traffic. *Courtesy Republican-American archives*

RIGHT: Exchange Place in Waterbury after a blizzard came through Waterbury February 19 and 20, 1934. *Courtesy Republican-American archives*

ABOVE: Hundreds of spectators gathered at the scene of the Waterbury-Winsted train wreck near Castle Bridge, January 23, 1929. *Courtesy Republican-American archives*

LEFT: Workers attempt to raise the battered train after the Waterbury-Winsted wreck occurred near Castle Bridge, January 23, 1929. *Courtesy Republican-American archives*

127

ABOVE: Morning after a fire destroyed the Watertown Avenue Garage, February 1936. *Courtesy Republican-American archives*

ABOVE: East Main Street is cleared after the blizzard left folks unable to get around Waterbury in February 1934. *Courtesy Republican-American archives*

LEFT: Bank Street looking north after a blizzard came through Waterbury, February 19 and 20, 1934. *Courtesy Republican-American archives*

RIGHT: Citizens on Congress Avenue, Waterbury, dig out after a storm hit the area July 6, 1935. *Courtesy Republican-American archives*

RIGHT: On April 8, 1935, tragedy struck as a fire destroyed the Middlebury Town Hall and Congregational Church. This view is from the rear while the blaze was in progress. The town hall is in the foreground and the church at right.
Courtesy Republican-American archives

BELOW: Only a few beams of the 96-year-old Congregational Church remained by the time four Waterbury and one Naugatuck Company and the Middlebury volunteer fire companies conquered the disastrous blaze. Fire Marshal Dennis J. Lahey is shown at left and Fire Captain Martin Campion is the man in the center. The man at right is believed to be one of Middlebury volunteers.
Courtesy Republican-American archives

BOTTOM RIGHT: Debris, twisted girders, chimneys and the brick covered vault are all that remain of Middlebury Town Hall, 1935. *Courtesy Republican-American archives*

RIGHT: Arthur Hivon passed in front of State Trooper Thomas F. Laden on his way into the Cheshire Town Hall for questioning, September 1937. He admitted to shooting and clubbing his wife Josephine to death after she instituted divorce proceedings against him a few weeks earlier.
Courtesy Republican-American archives

BELOW: State and local authorities search the area where bullets were found belonging to Arthur Hivon, September 14, 1937 after his wife was found slain. The troopers, from left: Harry Ritchie and Norman Davis. Constables are Wesley Collins, Leslie Hubbell and Leroy Carpenter.
Courtesy Republican-American archives

ABOVE: State Troopers, Norman Davis (left) and Harry Ritchie with Constables Leslie Hubbell (pointing), LeRoy Carpenter and Wesley Collins on railroad tracks where bloodhounds lost Hivon's trail after he murdered his wife in September 1937. *Courtesy Republican-American archives*

BELOW: A New Haven freight train is stopped by police in the vicinity of the Hivon murder. State troopers flagged the train hoping the crew would be able to tell them the whereabouts of Arthur Hivon, a fugitive. Hivon was eventually apprehended in Hamden a few days after the murder.
Courtesy Republican-American archives

ABOVE: A hurricane caused damage to this home and tree on Harpers Ferry Road in Waterbury. The hurricane swept through Connecticut on Wednesday afternoon September 21, 1938. The WPA helped with clean-up efforts throughout the state after the hurricane caused extensive damage and flooding. *Courtesy Republican-American archives*

LEFT: Cheshire school bus and oil truck accident, September 17, 1937. Fourteen students were injured and two died. *Courtesy Republican-American archives*

ABOVE: Terryville cider mill on South Main Street, was demolished in July 1937, when a windstorm swept through the area. *Courtesy Republican-American archives*

LEFT: The September 21, 1938 hurricane that swept through Connecticut and the area caused damage to trees and buildings as seen in this photo on Wolcott Street in Waterbury. The hurricane damage was heaviest at coastal locations in Connecticut.

Courtesy Republican-American archives

CHAPTER ELEVEN

Celebrations Well Attended

"What good is sitting alone in your room?
Come hear the music play.
Life is a Cabaret, old chum, Come to the Cabaret.
Put down the knitting, the book and the broom.
Time for a holiday.
Life is Cabaret, old chum, Come to the Cabaret.
Come taste the wine, Come hear the band.
Come blow your horn, Start celebrating; Right this way,
Your table's waiting."

— From "Cabaret," 1966

One certainty of the early years of the 20th century: If there was a worthwhile event, nearly the entire town would turn out.

Without the plethora of entertainment options that exist today, a parade, a dedication, a show or a sporting event would attract thousands. And something like a presidential appearance or a national figure arriving in town would mean even more.

Parade viewing was a major spectator sport, whether it be Memorial Day, St. Patrick's Day or any number of events.

Fairs in Terryville, Goshen, Bethlehem and Harwinton were always popular, and made for a nice fall ride in the country.

Without ubiquitous television and the plethora of entertainment now delivered by computer, civic events, sports and live entertainment were the basics of recreation throughout the region.

LEFT: Massed colors of the veterans organizations led the veterans division during the 1935 St. Patrick's Parade in Waterbury. *Courtesy Republican-American archives*

RIGHT: Memorial Day celebration near the Soldier's Monument, West Main, Waterbury, circa 1929. *Courtesy Republican-American archives*

LEFT: This Union City group prepares to take its place in a holiday parade, in Naugatuck circa 1920. *Courtesy Ron Gagliardi*

ABOVE: Swedish Viking float during Waterbury's 250th anniversary parade travels by Crosby High School, June 7, 1924. The week-long celebration began on June 2 with ceremonies at the Industrial and Mercantile Exposition in the State Armory on Field Street.
Courtesy Republican-American archives

RIGHT: Policemen march in a town parade on North Main Street, Waterbury, November 1923.
Courtesy Republican-American archives

ABOVE: Lieut. James Mulville leading the group of policemen during Waterbury's 250th anniversary parade, June 7, 1924. *Courtesy Republican-American archives*

LEFT: The Waterbury Republican clown contest parade, 1929.
Courtesy Republican-American archives

ABOVE: World War I Veterans march past the Scovill Mfg. Co. during Waterbury's 250th anniversary parade, June 7, 1924.
Courtesy Republican-American archives

RIGHT: Performers entertain a large crowd at the Wolcott Fair, 1928.
Courtesy Republican-American archives

LEFT: Harrub Memorial exercises, October 11, 1930. This monument was a memorial to the Pilgrim Heritage and Rhoby Smith Harrub, wife of Charles H. Harrub, chief engineer at the Waterbury Brass Co. He lived a frugal and quiet life and retired at the age of 75 to take care of his invalid wife. Rhoby died in 1921 and Charles died three years later at the age of 89. After his wife's death he set up a fund, selected a commission to see the monument was completed and picked the top American sculptor of the day, Herman Atkins MacNeil of New York and Paris. The 175-ton granite monument was moved from the foot of Chase Parkway in June 1964.
Courtesy Republican-American archives

RIGHT: Winners from Terryville in the hose laying competition in action during Watertown's 150th anniversary celebrations in June 1930.
Courtesy Republican-American archives

ABOVE: Memorial Day parade, Waterbury, 1930. *Courtesy Republican-American archives*

LEFT: National Guard marches in Waterbury Memorial Day Parade, 1930.
Courtesy Republican-American archives

ABOVE: The start of a parade at the Terryville Fair, 1930s. *Courtesy Republican-American archives*

RIGHT: Children of Mary St. Stanislaus Kostki Church, Waterbury, march in a parade celebrating Connecticut's Tercentennary, September 1935. *Courtesy Republican-American archives*

ABOVE: An auction at the fair in Bethlehem, 1930s. *Courtesy Republican-American archives*

LEFT: Watertown horse races, August 13, 1933. *Courtesy Republican-American archives*

LEFT: Harwinton Fair draws a large crowd in October 1936. *Courtesy Republican-American archives*

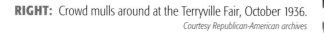

ABOVE: A team of oxen pulls a heavy load at the Bethlehem Fair, October 1936.
Courtesy Republican-American archives

RIGHT: Crowd mulls around at the Terryville Fair, October 1936.
Courtesy Republican-American archives

LEFT, ABOVE & RIGHT: An estimated 20,000 people turned out at Library Park in Waterbury on October 22, 1936 to hear President Franklin D. Roosevelt deliver a presidential campaign speech that lasted about five minutes. *Courtesy Republican-American archives*

RIGHT: Lieut. James Mulville lead this group of police officers during the 1936 St. Patrick's Day parade in Waterbury. *Courtesy Republican-American archives*

ABOVE: VFW Parade in Waterbury, June 19, 1937. *Courtesy Republican-American archives*

LEFT: Prominent city and state officials sit in the reviewing stand at City Hall during the 1936 St. Patrick's Day festivities in Waterbury. *Courtesy Republican-American archives*

Celebrations Well Attended